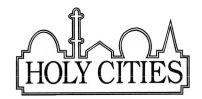

MECCA

Shahrukh Husain

Dillon Press
New York

First American publication 1993 by Dillon Press, Macmillan
Publishing Company, 866 Third Avenue, New York, NY
10022

Macmillan Publishing Company is part of the Maxwell
Communication Group of Companies.

First published by Evans Brothers Limited, 2A Portman
Mansions, Chiltern Street, London W1M 1LE

Printed in Hong Kong by Wing King Tong Co. Ltd.

10 9 8 7 6 5 4 3 2 1

ISBN 0–87518–572–X
Library of Congress Catalog Card Number 93–72324

For Monty and Samira

ACKNOWLEDGMENTS

Editorial: Catherine Chambers and Jean Coppendale
Design: Monica Chia
Production: Jenny Mulvanny

Maps: Jillian Luff of Bitmap Graphics

The author and publishers would like to thank:
Saviour Pirotta for his help in devising the Holy Cities
series.

For permission to reproduce copyright material the author
and publishers gratefully acknowledge the following:

Front cover: Main photograph – Pilgrims at the Kaaba
during the festival of Id-ul-Fitr – Peter Sanders, Trip; inset
left – A Muslim woman during the hajj (pilgrimage) – Peter
Sanders, Trip; inset right – Modern apartments in Mecca –
Peter Sanders, Trip

Back cover: Muslims praying around the Kaaba – Peter
Sanders, Trip

Endpapers: Front – Thousands of pilgrims on their way to
the Kaaba during the hajj – M. Biber, Robert Harding Picture
Library; Back – A decorated cover of the Koran – Robert
Harding Picture Library

Title page: A decorated copy of the Koran made in the 18th
century from Egypt – Trip

page 6 – (top) Tony Souter, Hutchison Library, (bottom)
Trip; page 7 – Trip; page 8 – (top) Tony Souter, Hutchison
Library, (middle) Trip, (bottom) Helene Rogers, Trip; page 9
– Trip; page 10 – (top) Trip, (bottom) Trip; page 11 – Trip;
page 12 – Trip; page 13 – (top) Trip, (middle) Trip, (bottom)
Juliet Highet, Hutchison Library; page 14 – Robert Harding
Picture Library; page 15 – (top) Robert Harding Picture
Library, (bottom) Trip; page 16 – Trip; page 17– Robert
Harding Picture Library; page 18 – Trip; page 19 – Trip; page
20 – Trip; page 21 – Trip; page 22 – Trip; page 23 – (top) Trip,
(bottom) Bob Turner, Trip; page 24 – Robert Harding Picture
Library; page 25 – (top) Trip, (middle) Trip, (bottom) Robert
Harding Picture Library; page 26 – (top) Robert Harding
Picture Library, (middle) Trip, (bottom) Trip; page 27 – Trip;
page 28 – Trip; page 29 – Trip; page 30 – Trip; page 31 – Trip;
page 32 – Trip; page 33 – Trip; page 34 – Trip; page 35 – Trip;
page 36 – (top) Trip, (middle and bottom) Helene Rogers,
Trip; page 37 – Helene Rogers, Trip; page 38 – (top) Tony
Souter, Hutchison Library, (bottom) Trip; page 39 – Trip;
page 40 – Trip; page 41 – Trip; Page 42 – (main picture)
Robert Harding Picture Library, (inset) John Egan,
Hutchison Library; page 43 – Trip; page 44 – (left) Hutchison
Library, (right) Trip.

Contents

Muslims usually say the words "peace be upon him" (*pbuh*) after they say the Holy Prophet Muhammad's name. These words have been left out of this text only for simplicity.

In the text, the letters C.E. are used after a year instead of A.D. For Muslims, they mean "the modern age," or the years after the birth of Jesus Christ. So, for instance, 1200 C.E. is the same as A.D. 1200.

A.H. after a year means "the years after the Hegira," when the Prophet Muhammad fled from Mecca to Medina. The Hegira marks the beginning of the Muslim calendar.

The meanings of the words in **bold** can be found in the **Key words** sections at the end of each chapter.

The magnetic city

Five times each day, millions of people all over the world turn toward Mecca to pray. They are Muslims, followers of the **Prophet** Muhammad. No matter where they live, they turn to face a holy building called the Kaaba, as God instructed through the Prophet. Their five daily prayers are called *salat*.

It was in Mecca that the Prophet Muhammad was born and where he received the powerful message that has influenced millions of people for more than 1,300 years. Where is this city that is so important to so many people?

A city of contrast

Mecca is 118 miles east of Jeddah, in the western province of Saudi Arabia. The city is surrounded by desert and bordered on the north, west, and south by spectacular mountain ranges. Three mountain passes lead into the city.

Mecca is a city of great variety. Its modern constructions contrast with one of the oldest surviving buildings in the world. The city is criss-crossed with a network of highways. A large roundabout encircles the religious buildings that dominate Mecca. The largest of

these is the Kaaba, surrounded by the Great **Mosque**. Today, these are enclosed by a large wall. At each corner of the wall, a **minaret** rises toward the sky. The four minarets are the tallest structures in the city.

This area, the heart of Mecca, is known as the Sacred Enclosure or the Holy Haram. The Kaaba has been the center of the community since the beginning. Its buildings, streets, and bazaars fan out around it in widening circles as far as the slopes of the surrounding hills.

The Kaaba itself stands in the lowest part of the Valley of Ibrahim in which Mecca is situated. It has been a place of worship for thousands of years. The Kaaba is 50 feet tall with a flat roof. It is built of stone and is roughly rectangular in shape, being taller than it is wide. On one side is a brass door decorated with religious verses. This is set well above the ground to prevent flood damage. Inside the Kaaba are three pillars that hold it up.

The Kaaba has always been a place of worship, though not always of the One God. For many years it was used by those who believed in many different gods and goddesses. Today, only Muslims can enter Mecca to see this greatest symbol of **monotheism**.

Here is the story of the remarkable city of Mecca through the ages.

Mecca nestles among the hills, with the Kaaba at its center. ▼

Key words

Prophet the messenger of God

mosque Muslim place of worship

minaret a tower from which a crier (muezzin) calls Muslims to prayer

monotheism belief in one God

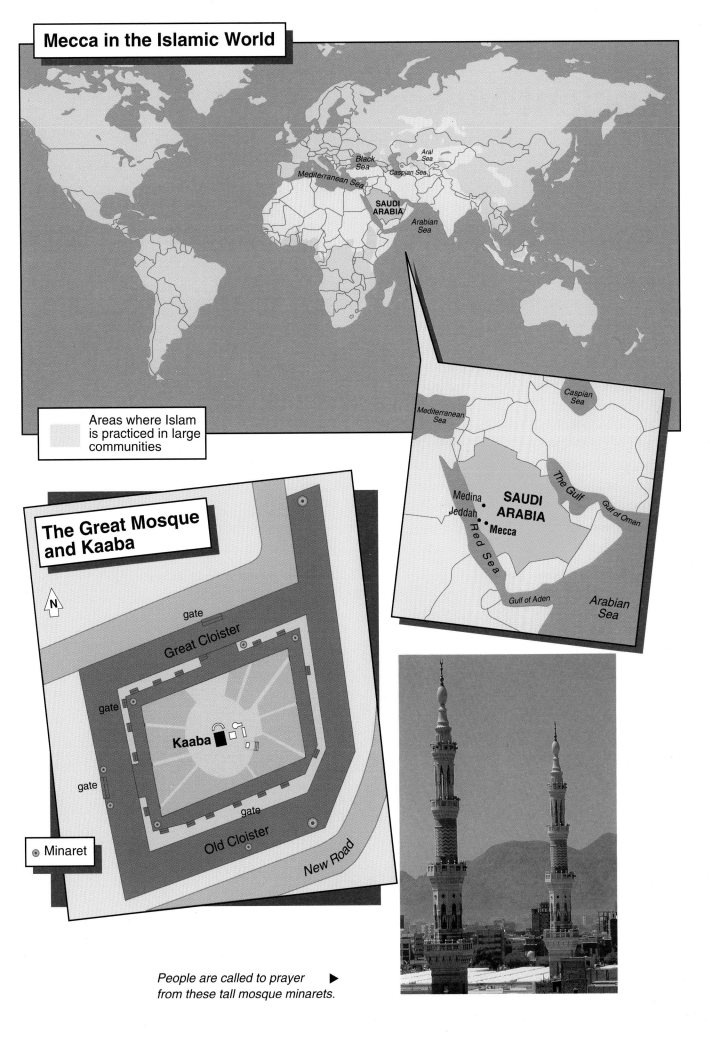

Mecca in the Islamic World

Black Sea
Aral Sea
Mediterranean Sea
Caspian Sea
SAUDI ARABIA
Arabian Sea

Areas where Islam is practiced in large communities

Mediterranean Sea
Caspian Sea
Medina
Jeddah
Mecca
SAUDI ARABIA
The Gulf
Gulf of Oman
Red Sea
Gulf of Aden
Arabian Sea

The Great Mosque and Kaaba

N

gate

Great Cloister

gate

gate

Kaaba

gate

gate

Old Cloister

New Road

◉ Minaret

People are called to prayer ▶
from these tall mosque minarets.

Ancient Mecca

Once, long ago, according to the Muslim holy book, God spoke to the Prophet Ibrahim. He told Ibrahim to take his wife Hajra and their baby son Ismail out to the desert and leave them between two small hills, Al-Safa and Al-Marwa. As always, Ibrahim followed God's command. After a while the baby became thirsty and ill from the intense heat. Hajra knew he needed water, but where was she to find it in the desert? She ran helplessly up and down between the hills, praying for a miracle. Suddenly, she saw water bubbling out of the earth and gurgling on to the sand by the baby's feet. The stream gushed water for as long as Hajra and Ismail needed it. The spring became known as Zam-zam. Its fame spread far and wide among the desert tribes, and people began to stop at the new oasis. Some settled there to be near the water. After Hajra died, Ibrahim returned to the spot.

Here with the help of his son, he built the Kaaba. This was a **monument** to the worship of the One and Only God, whom both Ibrahim and Ismail worshiped. Embedded in one corner of the Kaaba was a mysterious ancient black stone (see pages 29-30).

Time passed and Ismail grew up and married a daughter of the desert tribe of

▲ Dry desert hills in Saudi Arabia

▼ An oasis attracts passing travelers.

The spice route

Rich merchants traveled through Mecca all year-round with their camel caravans of goods. The most popular were the **aromatic** spices from the East, so the trade circuit became known as the Spice Route. The people of Mecca were themselves very good merchants and the visiting caravans did a brisk local trade. But foreign merchants also had to pay a caravan tax, an **import** tax, an **export** tax, and a sales tax on local sales. Mecca was an expensive trading station. Meccans earned money providing services to the merchant travelers. Innkeepers and other local traders were kept especially busy. Some Meccans learned mathematics and writing in order to provide accounting and record-keeping services for the merchants.

▲ *Busy traders in a small town market*

Jurhum, which had settled in Mecca. Ismail and his wife had 12 sons, who made 12 Arab tribes. Ismail remained by the Kaaba, guarding it all his life. But his descendants were eventually forced out by the Amalekites, a ferocious **pagan** tribe. Even pagan Arabs who had settled near the Kaaba must have felt its spiritual power, for they also used it as a place of worship. But their focus of worship was not the One and Only God, and gradually, the pagans filled the Kaaba with **idols**.

Hidden away in the mountains, in the center of the land called Hijaz, this crescent-shaped oasis of Mecca became a magnet to settlers, travelers, and traders. Apart from the pure and plentiful supply of water from Zam-zam, Mecca was attractive for two other reasons. First, hundreds of pagans poured into Mecca to visit the Kaaba. Second, two important trade routes passed through the city. One connected Africa to Asia and the other linked the East to the Mediterranean.

The black temple

In the years leading up to the birth of the Prophet Muhammad there were 360 pagan images in the Kaaba, roughly one for each day of the year. Hubal, Isaf, and Naila were the most important ones. Some pilgrims worshiped stones of unusual shapes and colors because they thought the greater gods were too important for them. There were two pilgrimage seasons, spring and autumn, which lasted two months each. People flocked to the Kaaba from far and wide to worship. During the four months set aside for the pilgrimage, fighting was forbidden.

While the pilgrims were in Mecca they spent freely and willingly. This, too, was good for local business. So Mecca prospered and gradually became the envy of its neighbors both within Arabia and outside. It was this wealth and opportunity that caused people to use the term "Mecca" to describe any place of success and plenty. It is still used in the English language today.

▲ *A woman in a farming community grinds cereal.*

▼ *Water gushes into a village water tank.*

The desert tribes

The Arabs of Hijaz were split into many different tribes that fought each other regularly. These desert people, known as Bedouin, were dotted all over the Middle East. They lived in the mountain ranges, the deserts, and the outskirts of cities such as Mecca. Most tribes followed the same laws and customs. The most important of these was **hospitality**. Men could die from thirst and sunstroke in the searing desert heat. Hospitality ensured that traveling tribesmen always had water and a resting place on their travels. So people were expected to offer food and shelter to anyone who asked, even a dangerous criminal. If this meant that the **host** might have to sacrifice his life or property to protect his guest, then he had to be ready and willing to do so. If all was peaceful, he was expected to let his guest stay at least three days. Then he would send him on his way with plenty to eat and drink.

Though the Bedouin constantly fought one

10 —

▲ *Two camels from a camel caravan*

another, they had agreements about most matters relating to daily life. Their laws told them how to fight, how to treat their prisoners, and how to punish offenders. They also had agreements about where their camels, cattle, goats, and sheep could graze freely. The Bedouin felt it was extremely important to be strong and brave.

These **nomadic** tribesmen did not have farms or land, so there was nothing to hold them in one place. Their lives were tough but free. They traveled from place to place

alone or with their tribes, settling where and when it suited them. Occasionally they raided and plundered towns and villages. Often they took work as caravan guides or traveling herdsmen. Some hired themselves out as fighters, staying away from their families for long periods of time. This helped them to earn a living, especially during a drought, when their goats and sheep suffered in the arid desert.

The citizens of Mecca

In contrast with the Bedouin nomads, the citizens of Mecca were settled and prosperous. The city was ruled by a council of elders. Usually they employed **mercenaries** from the Bedouin or slave-soldiers from Abyssinia (now Ethiopia) to fight their battles. But the men of Mecca were still desert tribesmen at heart, and they were ready to do battle themselves if necessary. Most Meccans were quite wealthy, so they could afford to hire workers from outside, mainly from Africa.

In the years directly before the birth of the Prophet Muhammad, the tribe of Quraysh was one of the most important in Mecca. Its

▼ *Camel harnesses inside a Bedouin tent*

chief, Abdul Muttaleb, was the head of the Mecca council of elders. This did not mean that his powers were unlimited. The people of Mecca had a system of local government that stopped any one person or group of people from becoming too powerful.

Some women played an important part in this society. Sometimes they were trained to take part in fighting. One Arab tribeswoman, named Zenobia, hired Roman mercenaries and became queen of Palmyra. She spoke Greek and crowned herself Augusta in 270 C.E. But more often, women were content to do business and be involved in the welfare of the town. Some famous women merchants of the time were Khadija, who later married the Prophet Muhammad, and Hind, who sold her merchandise to Syria.

Meccans were used to a luxurious life-style but they did not want to forget their nomadic roots. Parents often sent their sons to live with Bedouin women as soon as they were born. Bedouin women suckled the Meccan babies alongside their own children. Later, they were brought up in the desert, tending cattle and learning the ways of the desert. The links that Meccan boys made with the Bedouin tribes lasted forever.

The culture of the desert

The sons of the rich grew up in the healthier climate of the higher, more open regions around Mecca, away from the dust and heat of the lower desert. They learned the rules of tribal brotherhood and absorbed the loyalty, honor, and bravery that kept the tribes from wiping each other out. They became skilled in the art of desert survival: riding and using the sword. Gradually, they began to know the desert and its routes. They also mastered another art important to the Bedouin, composing and reciting verse. Their poems were long and rhythmic, telling stories of war, love, and history. Some poets described the glories of their tribes, while others wrote verse criticizing politicians. The Bedouin

loved poetry and set high standards for it. Bedouin verse forms are still used today and some original poetry still survives.

Key words

monument a construction that is built to honor a person or an event

pagan a person who believes in more than one god

idols statues at which people worship

aromatic sweet or strong smelling

import to bring goods into a country from abroad

export to send out goods from a country for sale abroad

hospitality generosity toward guests

host someone who receives a guest into his or her home

nomadic constantly moving from one place to another

mercenaries soldiers who fight for money, not for a cause

Which Way Do We Go?

For Bedouins, moving is a way of life. To cross the desert, they practice an art known as transhumance. This involves using trees, rocks, the stars, and other natural landmarks to navigate a series of trails laid out centuries ago by their ancestors. Each group of Bedouins has a set pattern of migration, which they pass down from generation to generation.

The Messenger

In the years prior to the Holy Prophet's birth, Mecca was at the height of its success. The spice trade was thriving. The caravans of Mecca were famous for their fabulous wealth. From Mecca, they carried leather, currants from neighboring Taif, and silver and gold **ingots** as well as gold dust. The most popular goods were perfumes, aromatic tree gum, and medicines, including the famous senna of Mecca, which is still used today. Returning caravans brought home silk, slaves, weapons, cereals, and oil. The caravans of Mecca boasted profits of 100 percent. Their return and departure was a great event in the city because almost everyone was involved in the trade in some way. Even though the traders

▲ *Gold jewelry in a shop window*

◀ *Raisins drying on a mat*

Herbs and spices in a marketplace ▼

hired guards for protection, desert tribes often tried to plunder their riches.

The threat to the Kaaba

Kings of other countries wanted a share in these riches. But luckily, Mecca was well protected by mountain ranges and the sea.

To the north, the Byzantine emperor carefully watched Mecca's rising fortunes. To the northeast, the emperor of Persia anxiously looked on, worried that the wealth and power of Hijaz might pose a threat to his empire. Across the Red Sea, the king of Abyssinia was concerned that the tribes of the Hijaz would unite and rise to destroy them all. So neighboring kings made sure that the tribes of Hijaz were always busy fighting one another. That way they would remain safe.

In 570 C.E. Abraha, the Christian Abyssinian king of Yemen, attacked Mecca. He wanted a share of Mecca's spice trade and its wealth. He also wanted to take Christianity to the Kaaba. The holy monument was attracting the followers of yet another religion.

Abraha crossed the desert with his army of soldiers and elephants and surrounded Mecca. He ordered the Meccans to surrender but they refused. The Kaaba, they said, belonged to the One God, and they were its guardians. Abraha gave his elephants the order to storm the city. As they began their charge, an act of God saved the Meccans. It seemed as if swarms of small birds filled the sky, hailing down small, hard stones on Abraha's army. The great beasts collapsed to their knees. Abraha was frightened by this miracle and immediately retreated to his country. This story illustrates how closely God has been connected with Mecca from the beginning of time. The Meccans named this the Year of the Elephant.

The most precious gift

This miraculous gift from heaven to Mecca was followed by a greater and more lasting one. Around this time, Amina, a woman of a **clan** called the Hashemites, was expecting a baby. The Hashemites were part of the wealthy and powerful tribe of Quraysh. Amina's husband, Abdullah, was the son of Abdul Muttaleb, the ruler of Mecca. Sadly, Abdullah died before the baby was born. After her husband died, Amina was not well off, nor was she in good health.

In 571 C.E. she gave birth to a boy. She named her son Muhammad. In keeping with the custom of the time, Amina gave Muhammad to a Bedouin woman, Haleema, to bring up. Muhammad stayed with

Young boys with herds of ► *sheep and goats*

Haleema for four years. He learned from the Bedouin their generosity and hospitality, qualities that remained vital to him all his life.

Two years after Muhammad's return to Mecca, when he was only six, his mother died. His uncle Abu Taleb gave him all the love and protection he needed.

The Holy Prophet

Muhammad was tall, well built, and very energetic. He was often seen on the streets and slopes in and around Mecca walking so fast that his companions could not keep up with him. He was light-skinned and had light brown eyes. His hair and beard were thick and slightly curly. Though he spoke clearly and fast, he was not a man of many words. He loved children and was kind to animals and often told people not to upset them. This kindness was an important part of his character.

▲ *A Bedouin boy with his father*

Even as a small boy Muhammad spent a lot of time **meditating**. He was a very honest boy and earned the nickname Al-Amin—The Truthful—when he was still very young. When he was in his teens, Abu Taleb found him a job on the caravan of a **widowed** businesswoman, Khadija. She was so impressed with Muhammad that she asked him to marry her, even though she was 15 years older. Muhammad accepted her proposal and they lived happily together and had six children. Sadly, the couple's sons died when they were still young but they adopted a slave boy, Zaid bin Harith. Their four daughters grew up and married important people around Mecca. One of them, Fatimah, married Ali, son of Abu Taleb, Muhammad's uncle. It is through her that the Prophet's **line** continues.

Key words

ingots molded shapes of pure metal

clan a group of families with a single chief

meditating thinking deeply

widow a woman whose husband has died

line describes an unbroken family of descendants

The Message

In the year 612 C.E. when Muhammad was about 40, he spent a great deal of time in a cave on Hira, one of the many mountains that surround Mecca. He went there to think deeply about life, because the spiritual need he felt as a child had become even stronger. One day as Muhammad was meditating, he saw the Angel Gabriel who had a message from God. Muhammad was to tell the people of Mecca that there was just one God, Allah, and that they should worship only Him. This occurred during the last ten days of Ramadan, the ninth month of the Islamic **lunar calendar**. There is a festival to mark this event (see page 36). Muhammad began to preach the message and God continued to use Muhammad as His messenger.

The **injunctions** that came down to Muhammad in Mecca were usually short and clear. Mostly they described God as the Supreme Power who was All-Merciful and All-Forgiving. Through Gabriel, God told Muhammad about the prophets of the past, such as Moses, Abraham, and Jesus. He also told him about life after death, which the Jewish and especially the Christian visitors to Mecca had spoken of.

The words of God were often like poetry, rhythmic and flowing. Sometimes the phrases rhymed. Muhammad's followers wrote these verses down wherever they could in order to memorize them exactly. Some were written down on **parchment**, others on stone or the bark of trees. Yet others were memorized by the Prophet's companions.

The most important message was very simple. All those who believed Muhammad's message had to say clearly:

> *"There is no God but Allah, and*
> *Muhammad is the Messenger of Allah."*

These words became known as the *shahada*.

Trials and tribulations

The first people to accept Muhammad's message were his wife Khadija and his cousin Ali. He preached also to his mother's clan, the Hashemites (see page 14). Many clan members also accepted the message. The believers became known as Muslims, which means "They who surrender to God." A few of the Meccan **elite**, like Muhammad's uncle Abu Taleb, respected Muhammad, although they did not accept the message. But most wealthy Meccans were angry with Muhammad because he preached that their gods were false. Also, if too many people believed what Muhammad said, the Kaaba would lose its importance, and Meccans would no longer be respected as the keepers

◄ *Mount Hira, where the Holy Prophet spent a lot of time in prayer and meditation*

▲ *Jerusalem is now the third most important city to Muslims. The large golden dome is part of the building known as the Dome of the Rock.*

of Kaaba. The money gained from pilgrims to the city would be lost as well.

Many of the earliest Muslims were slaves and laborers. Their masters became angry and tried to stop them practicing their new religion, Islam. The believers were tortured, locked up, and in some cases, killed. In spite of this they did not give up their new faith.

Muhammad was downhearted when he saw how much his followers were suffering for the sake of their beliefs. Then his wife, Khadija, died. She had been his greatest comfort, giving him strength and courage during his most difficult moments. Muhammad mourned her death deeply. A while later his uncle Abu Taleb also died. He had always supported Muhammad, protecting him and his followers when others had turned against them. With all this grief and with continued threats against his followers, Muhammad felt that it was time to leave Mecca. At that time a group of men from the neighboring city of Yathrib invited Muhammad to come and preach to them. He accepted their invitation and sent his

companions ahead, and promised to follow them when they were safe.

In the year 622 C.E., still in danger of his life, the Prophet kept his promise. Along with his dear friend Abu-Bakr, he left for Yathrib. His presence in Yathrib later made the city world famous by the name of Medina. Muhammad's departure from Mecca to Medina is known as Hegira —the emigration. Muslims chose this as the starting point of their calendar. This became known as year 1 of the Hegira —generally written as 1 A.H.

Key words

lunar calendar the calendar that follows the cycle of the moon; each month is 29 or 30 days

injunctions orders

parchment paper made from animal skin

elite leaders and ruling class

Medina, city of light

The city of Yathrib was built on a plateau 2,000 feet above sea level. Volcanic rocks surrounded it. The climate was pleasant for most of the year, although the summers were very hot. Water and grass were plentiful. Date palms and other fruit trees grew well on its fertile soil and the land around Yathrib was used for farming. This was very different from the parched, barren environment of Mecca.

The mighty Christian Byzantine empire stood to the north of Yathrib, but the city was well protected from attack by the fortresses built around it.

The story goes that when Muhammad arrived in Yathrib, many people offered him hospitality and land. But the Prophet did not wish to be a burden to anyone. Nor did he want anyone to feel that he favored one person over another. So Muhammad

announced that he would build a house for himself on the spot where his camel decided to stop. The people followed Muhammad and his camel eagerly, waiting for the animal to settle down. She eventually sat down to rest on an open piece of land. The owners were willing to sell the land. Muhammad bought it, and with his companions soon began to build a house. As they worked, Muhammad's helpers sang a song.

*"If we sit down when the Prophet works
It may be said that we have shirked."*

Others chanted God's praise and the Prophet joined in their chanting.

The Mosque of the Prophet

Muhammad's house was neither grand nor large. Its walls were 10 feet tall and built of mud bricks. The roof was held up by the trunks of palm trees, and thatched with palm leaves bonded together with mud. It was built around an open courtyard about 180

Ancient Mecca (left) and Medina (right) are depicted in this beautifully decorated book. ▼

Top: *Building a house using local stone*

▲ *The Mosque of the Prophet in Medina*

◄ *A baked clay mosque in El Gassim*

square feet. Part of this was carpeted. Muhammad received his visitors and companions in this area. It was also from here that he led the *salat* five times a day. Those without homes found shelter here. No traveler was ever turned away, even though Muhammad and his family often had nothing more to eat than a few dates and a little milk. Two cabins were built alongside this simple house. Around this time Muhammad and Abu-Bakr sent for their families. Muhammad married again, to Ayesha, the young daughter of Abu-Bakr. Ayesha moved into one of the cabins.

The buildings became known as the Mosque of the Prophet, the second mosque of Islam. The first was built at Qubaa, outside Medina, but it is the second that houses Muhammad's grave. When it was first built it had three doors. The faithful prayed facing the direction of Jerusalem, the holy city of the Jews and the Christians. A year later, God

▲ *The city of Medina as it is today*

told the Prophet that Muslims should change the direction of their prayers to the Kaaba. Muhammad was also told that Muslims should go as pilgrims to the Kaaba for hajj (pilgrimage) at least once in their lives (see pages 29-33). Muhammad closed the door to Jerusalem and built a fourth door facing Mecca. Seven years later the mosque was enlarged.

Muhammad continued to receive messages from God while he was in Yathrib. During 623 C.E. (the first year of Hegira), God instructed him through the Angel Gabriel that the month of Ramadan should be set aside for fasting. This was to remind people that Ramadan was when Muhammad first received God's message. The first day of the following month of Shawwal would be set aside for a feast known as *Id-ul-Fitr*. Muslims still fast during the month of Ramadan, and celebrate the feast of *Id-ul-Fitr* at the end of it (see page 37).

Regaining Mecca

The new religion was growing stronger and more popular all the time. Meccans were not happy about this and were always plotting to make Muhammad and his followers look bad. Over the following years, a lot of fighting took place between the Meccans and the Muslims.

Muhammad was now well-settled in Yathrib, which was beginning to be known as *Madina-ul-Rasul*, the City of the Prophet. It was also known as *Medina Al-Munawwara*, the Enlightened City. This was because it was now the home of Muhammad, who had brought the Light of God's knowledge to the faithful. It was later known just as Medina. The Prophet's four closest friends and trusted advisers lived with him in Medina. They were Ali, Abu-Bakr, Omar, and Uthman. All of Muhammad's family and friends were in Medina with him. Yet he felt homesick for Mecca and often wondered how he could return. He knew from travelers that the people of Mecca were still hostile toward him.

Then in year 628 C.E. (6 A.H.), God told Muhammad that one day he would return triumphant to Mecca. Immediately, Muhammad gathered a group of followers and crossed the desert to the city of his birth.

▲ *Pilgrims flock to Mecca to take part in the hajj.*

The Meccans became nervous and made a treaty with him. The treaty allowed Muslims to return each year as pilgrims. Some time later they broke the agreement and Muhammad decided to take stronger action.

He organized a large army and returned to Mecca. The people of Mecca surrendered even before the fighting started. Muhammad ordered his men to disarm themselves. Then he entered the city and marched directly to the Kaaba. There he told the city elders that he had won Mecca for the Muslims by the Grace of God. He did not bear any grudges against the Meccans.

Islam unites Mecca

Muhammad spent the first few weeks purifying the Kaaba. He removed the idols from there and from other shrines of the Hijaz. Soon the local people became convinced that Muhammad spoke of a true God. It was not long before the different tribes of Mecca accepted Islam as their new religion. They were united as Muslims; revenge and hostility were put aside. Mecca became a united city—the holiest city of Islam.

The elders of Mecca asked Muhammad to make it his home once again, but he wished to return to Medina. Starting from the Kaaba he made a final visit to all the holy sites. He

traveled to the hills of Arafat, Muzdalifa, and Mina on the outskirts of Mecca, as he had done on all his previous pilgrimages. After two years of campaigning to spread Islam, Muhammad found that the battles had taken their toll on his health. He was still weary from his expedition when he developed a fever. On the 12th of the month of Rabi-ul-Awwal, June 7, 632 C.E. (10 A.H.) Muhammad died peacefully in the company of his wife, Ayesha. Muhammad was buried in Ayesha's home. A mosque was built over it, which is known as the Mosque of the Prophet (see page 19).

The Five Pillars of Islam

The Five Pillars of Islam are rules that all Muslims must obey. They come from the Prophet's message from God.

All Muslims must proclaim, "There is no God but Allah and Muhammad is the Messenger of Allah."

All Muslims should perform five sets of salat *each day.*

All Muslims should fast during the month of Ramadan, eating and drinking nothing between sunrise and sunset.

All Muslims should give alms (charity) calculated at 2.5 percent of their wealth.

All Muslims should make a pilgrimage to Mecca at least once in their lifetime.

▲ The oldest handwritten Koran was made in 1640 C.E.

◄ The Koran printing press in Medina

After the death of the Holy Prophet, his four chief companions took turns leading the Muslims. Like Muhammad, they preferred to lead the Muslim community from Medina rather than Mecca. Leaders were known as khalifas (caliphs). The first khalifa was Abu-Bakr. He was elected by the Muslim community immediately after the death of the Prophet in 632 C.E.

The Holy Koran

Omar took over from Abu Bakr in 634 C.E. but was assassinated in 644 C.E. During his ten years as khalifa, he achieved many important things. He made the prayer space larger around the Kaaba. To do this he bought and demolished the grand mansions around the

holy shrine. He also had a task for Zaid bin Thabit, the Prophet's secretary. Zaid was to collect the complete message that Muhammad had received from God. Some parts of the message had already been written down. Other parts had been memorized by the **faithful**, many of whom were now old and would not live long. Zaid had a difficult task ahead of him. He had to make sure that the verses were recorded exactly as the Holy Prophet had reported them. Finally by 656 C.E. the collection was completed and made into a book known as the Holy Koran. Uthman, who was khalifa at the time, allowed copies to be made. The Koran is highly respected by Muslims.

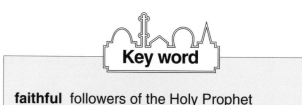

Key word

faithful followers of the Holy Prophet

The spread of Islam

From the central point of Mecca, deep in the Valley of Ibrahim, the message of Islam spread outside Arabia. Under Omar's leadership the Muslims conquered and **converted** Iraq, Jerusalem, Persia (Iran), and Egypt. Islam spread far and wide.

When Uthman was elected khalifa in 644 C.E., he found himself in charge of a large and growing Islamic empire. Uthman was murdered in 656 C.E. and was **succeeded** by Ali, the kinsman and son-in-law of the Holy Prophet. In 661 C.E., Ali was also assassinated, only five years after becoming khalifa.

Ali's successor was a member of the Omayyad clan, and a close relative of Uthman. With him, the **khilafat** became **hereditary** in the Omayyad family. They moved their capital to Damascus in Syria.

The Arab empire soon stretched from Spain in the west to Central Asia in the east.

Many Arabs left Arabia to settle in the new Muslim countries. Although it was no longer the political center of the empire, Arabia became even more important in a different way. It was now the country that held the holy cities of Islam. Mecca, especially, grew in importance. It became the spiritual heart for the peoples of more and more countries. But rebel groups wanted to become the rulers of the Muslim empire. Mecca was so important to Muslims that it became the target of military attacks.

The holy city was taken by rebels between 745 and 746 C.E. Just before this, the Omayyad khalifas were replaced by the Abbasid **dynasty** in 750 C.E. Instead of Damascus, the Abbasids chose Baghdad in Iraq as their capital. From this new center, the

Inside the mosque at Cordoba

▲ This stunning dome and minaret belong to a mosque in Baghdad, Iraq.

▲ Fine leatherwork has been used on this camel seat.

forces of Islam conquered more areas of Asia, eventually reaching India. But Mecca remained Islam's most holy city, to which pilgrims from the ever-expanding Muslim world were drawn.

Like all great empires, the Abbasid khilafat gradually fell apart. Many of the provinces of their empire were carved up into local kingdoms by Turkish warlords, who ruled them as sultans. These sultans were really independent but they always asked the khalifas to agree to their authority as Muslim rulers.

Eventually in 1258 C.E. the Abbasids lost their capital, Baghdad, to the Muslim Mongols from Asia. The last khalifa fled from these fierce invaders to the protection of the Mamluks. The Mamluks were a Turkish Muslim dynasty who ruled Egypt and also controlled Mecca and the rest of the Hijaz. The khalifas kept their contact with Mecca, although the Mamluks had the real power.

During this time the Mamluks used to send a special gift to Mecca each year. This was an elaborately made seat, strapped on to the back of a camel. It traveled by special caravan across the desert. The gift showed how much the Mamluks honored Mecca. This custom

was continued by the Ottomans, another dynasty of Turkish rulers who created one of the greatest Muslim empires. From their base in Turkey, the Ottomans conquered most of southeastern Europe. They established flourishing Muslim communities in countries such as Bosnia. In 1453 the Ottomans captured Constantinople from the last of the Byzantine emperors. They made it their capital and gave it the new name of Istanbul. From there, they conquered most of the Arab lands in the Middle East. The Mamluks held out until 1517 C.E., when they, too, were completely defeated by the Ottoman sultan, who added Egypt and the Hijaz to his empire.

The sultan forced the last of the Abbasid khalifas to give the title of khalifa to him. For 400 years, the Hijaz was ruled as a **province** of the Ottoman empire, with a governor appointed from Istanbul. The sultans showed great respect toward Mecca. They kept up the Mamluk custom of sending a cloth called the *Kiswa* (see pages 28 to 29) to cover the Kaaba each year. Under their protection, pilgrims continued to flock to Mecca each year. Not only did they come overland from the Middle East and Asia, but often made dangerous

journeys by sea from as far away as Indonesia, where Islam had now spread.

The Ottoman empire finally ended when the sultans joined in World War I (1914-1918). They were defeated, along with their allies, the Germans.

Recent history of Saudi Arabia

In 1932 the kingdom of Hijaz was renamed Saudi Arabia after its present rulers. Their ancestor, Saud Ibn Muhammad Ibn Migren, came from an ancient desert tribe that had ruled sections of the Hijaz at different times. He died in 1725. Mecca changed hands several times during those troubled centuries. In 1805 Saud's son, Muhammad, fought hard to protect Mecca from an invasion by Egypt and the Ottomans. He held it for four years before being captured and eventually executed. Other members of his dynasty

▲ *Inside the royal tent at the races—horse racing is a favorite royal sport*

▶ *King Fahd Ibn Abdul Aziz—the Custodian of the Mosque*

continued the struggle to protect Mecca and keep it as a center of true Muslim worship. In 1926 his descendant, Ibn Saud, was proclaimed king of Hijaz.

The present ruler of Saudi Arabia, Fahd Ibn Abdul Aziz, changed his title to Custodian of the Sacred Places (Mecca and Medina). He has banned people from addressing him as "Your Majesty" or "My Lord." He personally supervises improvements to the religious sites in and around Mecca.

▼ *The Blue Mosque in Istanbul, Turkey*

Key words

converted changed the beliefs of people

succeeded followed

khilafat the land and people ruled by a khalifa

hereditary passed down from parent to child

dynasty rulers who belong to the same family

province a separate region governed by rulers outside the area

Modern Mecca

In the 1970s a demand for oil grew around the world. Saudi Arabia is rich in oil resources, so a lot of oil was sold and money poured into Saudi Arabia. For Mecca this meant many changes. The city had looked the same for many years. Now it suddenly found itself in the middle of a major redevelopment program. The needs of the millions of pilgrims who flocked to Mecca greatly influenced the planning of the city. Pilgrims for *Umra*, a short pilgrimage, came throughout the year. But the strongest impact occurred during the main pilgrimage, hajj, when for two weeks each year, two million pilgrims gathered in Mecca. Somehow, more space had to be created for them.

Whole areas were pulled down around the center of Mecca. The people living there were resettled in new areas on its outskirts. These new **suburbs** made Mecca much larger. The old houses on the mountain slopes were also rebuilt. Bedouin tents disappeared and concrete houses appeared in their place, creating small villages. New roads connected the villages outward to neighboring cities and inward to the center of Mecca.

▼ *Buildings sprang up in Saudi Arabia in the 1970s.*

▲ *Modern buildings now surround the Holy Haram in the center of Mecca.*

***Top**: A network of oil pipes in Saudi Arabia*

Roads and transport

The whole of Mecca was revolutionized almost overnight. Where there had been dirt roads, large highways and overpasses appeared. Modern tunnels were blasted through the surrounding mountains. The difficult journeys over hills and through rocky routes and desert tracks were no longer needed.

The new suburbs and the large roads solved the main problems for pilgrims, creating more space and easing traffic. They also provided Meccans with a larger, more stylish city.

Public facilities

Redevelopment included a new health service for the people of Mecca and the pilgrims. New hospitals and health centers were built to look after them. Many of these centers are in the holy sites on the outskirts of Mecca. Cleanliness is an important part of Islam and the hajj as well as health and safety, but there had always been a water shortage in the desert city of Mecca. This is no longer a problem. Mecca is now well-supplied from Al-Shuaiba on the Red Sea, where huge desalination plants have been built. Here, the salt is removed from the sea-water to provide fresh water for drinking and washing.

Efficient public transportation and postal services have been set up. The Pilgrims' Postal Service sends mail to 43 Islamic states during the hajj period. Each week, 157 batches of mail are electronically sorted, stamped, and packed. Hajj **missions** and other local organizations deal with the domestic mail. All these services have created new jobs.

Mecca prepares for the hajj

There is no doubt that the hajj turns the lives of Meccans inside out. They have to hand their city over to pilgrims and offer them all the help they can. Although life is hard for Meccans during this period, they consider it an honor. They have grown up knowing that for the pilgrims the visit to Mecca means that their dream has come true. At this time, the roads have to be kept as clear as possible so that pilgrims and others can travel easily. This means that only cars with special permits can enter the city during the hajj period. Meccans have to park their cars outside the city and travel in on public transportation. The roads are constantly

▼ *Thousands of tents are supplied for pilgrims during the hajj. Here, they are being fireproofed for safety.*

▲ *Hajj guides prepare to lead pilgrims to a holy site.*

bustling with buses and busloads of pilgrims.

The local people make the best of all this. They have the chance to show their hospitality and to do good business. Hotels make sure they have prepared enough rooms for the thousands of guests. Markets are well stocked. Street sellers are constantly present around the Sacred Enclosure (the Great Mosque), selling cold drinks and things to eat. Pilgrims buy rosaries, prayer mats, and small Korans to use while they are on the hajj. Special booklets that explain everything about the hajj are on sale, too. Guides are often employed to lead pilgrims through the hajj in the proper manner. The guides come from families who have done this work for years.

There is excitement in the city as the pilgrimage month of Dhu'l-Hijja draws near and Mecca prepares to welcome the pilgrims, as it has for centuries.

Key words

suburbs living quarters outside the city

missions organizations set up to help people

City of grace

Pilgrims start arriving in Saudi Arabia from all over the world as Dhu'l Hijja (the hajj month) approaches (see page 27). They usually land at Jeddah airport. Once, the journey took several years. Today it can be covered in a few days or even hours. Air-conditioned buses or cars carry pilgrims from the airport into Mecca.

While in Mecca, the pilgrims stay in different places. Some can afford the luxury of five-star hotels; others camp out. It is not unusual to see a party of pilgrims spread a cloth on the pavement when the day is over and share food with one another. Some pilgrims have only paid for the fare to Mecca and have to earn their fare home. They bring goods from their own countries, which they sell on the streets outside the Sacred Enclosure, or Holy Haram, as it is also called. Others try to find work as laborers.

The hajj begins

Dressed in white and chanting the words *"Labbaika, Allah humma labbaik,"* which mean

▼ *A pilgrim sells jewelry to help pay for his hajj.*

▲ *Pilgrims pour through one of the gates of the Sacred Enclosure along a footbridge.*

"Here I am, Oh God, at your service," the pilgrims approach the holy site. They see the walls of the Sacred Enclosure. They admire the beauty of its towering minarets, longing to pass through its gates and allow their eyes to feast on the Kaaba.

The wall surrounding the Sacred Enclosure was built in 1955. It separates the religious area from the hustle and bustle of the city. The wall has four gates—Al-Fath, Al-Omra, King's Gate, and Al-Safa. The entire area within it is well-lit for night prayers. The pilgrims pour in through all four gates and admire the magnificent structure of the Kaaba clothed in its robe of black, which is known as the *Kiswa.*

The *Kiswa*

Under the various khilafats, the shrine of black stone was covered with the *kiswa*, a gigantic cloth. It was made of fine fabrics and colored the same as the flag of the khalifa in power. For many years the cloth was manufactured in Egypt. It was carried to Mecca by caravan and the journey took more than 40 days. Today it is made in Mecca by weavers and embroiderers whose families have done this work for many generations.

The *Kiswa* measures 2,578 square feet and weighs 2 tons. Much of its weight is made up by the pure gold used to embroider it. The

Far left: Weaving the cloth for the Kiswa

◀ *Embroidering the* Kiswa *with gold thread*

gold embroidery proclaims the *shahada* (**testimony**),

> *"There is no God but Allah and Muhammad is the Messenger of Allah."*

On the 25th of Dhu'l Qa'dah, the month before Dhu'l-Hijja on the Islamic calendar, the old *Kiswa* is removed in a special ceremony and given to the doorkeepers. They cut it into small pieces, which they sell as souvenirs of the hajj. The inside walls of the Kaaba are then covered in **inscriptions** from the Koran. Other than a few gold and silver

lamps hanging from the ceiling, the shrine is not decorated. On the 27th of Dhu'l-Hijja the custodian cleans the mosque in a special ceremony, and the new cloth is laid. Many worshipers are present.

The first step of the hajj

The first ritual of the hajj is to circle the Kaaba. Starting from a brownish-black stone embedded in a corner of the Kaaba, pilgrims do this seven times, moving in a counter-clockwise direction. The black stone bears its

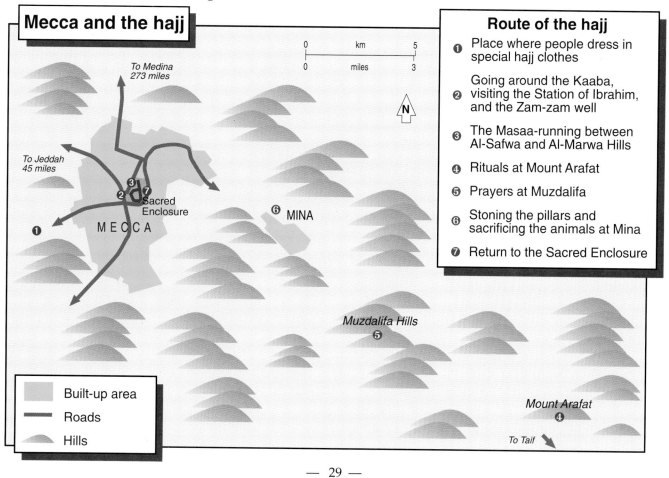

Mecca and the hajj

To Medina 273 miles

To Jeddah 45 miles

Sacred Enclosure

MECCA

⑥ MINA

Muzdalifa Hills
⑤

Mount Arafat
④

To Taif ↘

Built-up area
Roads
Hills

Route of the hajj

❶ Place where people dress in special hajj clothes

❷ Going around the Kaaba, visiting the Station of Ibrahim, and the Zam-zam well

❸ The Masaa-running between Al-Safwa and Al-Marwa Hills

❹ Rituals at Mount Arafat

❺ Prayers at Muzdalifa

❻ Stoning the pillars and sacrificing the animals at Mina

❼ Return to the Sacred Enclosure

▲ *Pilgrims clutch at the Kaaba and the* Kiswa.

own clues to its history, though no one knows for certain where it came from. It is said to have cracked in three places during a fire in 683 C.E. In 930 C.E. a group of zealots from the Persian Gulf marched across the desert. They invaded Mecca and massacred 50,000 people. Then they carried off the stone. It was returned in 951 C.E. It had been chipped since its removal and was reset in a silver band.

The Station of Ibrahim

Near the Kaaba is a case known as the Maqam Ibrahim (Station of Ibrahim). In it lies the boulder on which Ibrahim stood when he built the Kaaba. The Maqam was once a

▼ *Prayers are offered at the Maqam Ibrahim.*

building 50 feet long and held up by six pillars. It is now a small structure made of crystal. The stone, placed on a marble stand inside, is clearly visible through it. The pilgrims offer *salat* (prayers) there.

Zam-zam

After the pilgrims have completed their prayers at the Station of Ibrahim, they drink some water from the ancient well of Zam-zam. Until recently an enormous building covered and protected the well. This has been removed. A marble staircase now leads down to the well. Beneath Zam-zam is a cooling plant operated by an electronic computer system.

Al-Safa and Al-Marwa

▲ *On the runway between the hills of Al-Safa and Al-Marwa*

Beyond the clear, circular space around the Kaaba was once an open area filled with shops and traffic. This separated the Kaaba from the strip of desert where Hajra ran when seeking help for baby Ismail (see page 8). The dividing area has been cleared and paved. Now pilgrims can walk directly from the Kaaba to the Masaa (Hajra's strip of desert) without having to struggle past buildings and traffic.

The hills of Al-Safa and Al-Marwa are unrecognizable today. The pilgrims see no hills or stretches of desert here as they leave

▲ *Even today, some pilgrims perform the hajj on foot.*

◀ *Pilgrims fill hajj buses as they move between the holy sites.*

Zam-zam. Instead they find themselves in a two-story building about 1,300 feet long. They walk briskly up and down this air-conditioned area, which is divided into a two-way system. Stairs going up and down at each end represent the hills. The Masaa also has escalators and six bridges. Ramps and paths are reserved for wheelchairs. A duct in the roof of the Masaa diverts water from winter rains. This protects the Sacred Enclosure from floods, which have been a problem since ancient times.

When the pilgrims have completed their walk here, they prepare for the journey to Mina and Arafat.

Arafat

The granite hill of Mount Arafat, also known as the Jabl-al-Rehma (the Mount of Mercy), is about 40 miles east of Mecca. It is about 200 feet high with broad stone steps leading to the top. Once, pilgrims made the journey to Arafat by camel or on foot. Today, most travel in comfort in buses, coaches, and cars. When the pilgrims reach Mount Arafat they pitch camp, covering the hillside with thousands of tents. Fire precautions are

needed and hajj scouts patrol the area to make sure everyone is safe.

The part of the hajj known as the Main Pilgrimage begins here on the ninth day of the month of Dhu'l-Hijja. In the afternoon, the Hajjis (pilgrims) gather together to listen to the Arafat sermon. It is given from the 60th step. This is where the Holy Prophet preached a sermon on his last pilgrimage.

Two million pilgrims listen in silence in the sun of high noon. Afterward they chant *"Labbaik,"* say their prayers, and read the Koran. In the early evening they begin their walk to Muzdalifa.

▲ *Thousands of tents are pitched at Mount Arafat.*

▲ *Pilgrims gather around the mosque at Arafat.*

Muzdalifa

The pilgrims spend the night of the 9th of Dhu'l-Hijja in Muzdalifa, which is halfway between Arafat and Mina. This is another hilly spot, stretching away to the high mountain range of Taif. A mosque on the hill lights the pilgrims' way. Many have described their powerful emotions as they sit on the stones on the mountainside with nothing between them and the sky. The moon is nearly full at this time of the month, and in the deep of the night they see the desert lit only by the light of the moon and stars. The bare landscape stretches away in all directions between the surrounding mountains. Here, many pray through the night, leaving early the next morning for Mina.

Mina

The final stop of the Main Pilgrimage (hajj) is Mina. This lies on the way back to Mecca. It is a small town of stone houses surrounded by steep cliffs. Mina has a square mosque first built by the ruler Salahuddin (Saladin) in the 13th century. Three roughly carved stone pillars stand here to represent the devil. The pilgrims spend some time collecting small stones from the mountain slopes before they gather here. These stones are thrown at the pillars to show that Muslims are determined

Pilgrims gather for prayer at Mina. ▶

to reject the devil, as the Holy Prophet had done.

The hajj is now complete and the pilgrims celebrate *Id-al-Adha*, one of the two most important Muslim festivals. People bargain with local shepherds and tradesmen over the price of livestock. The animal sacrifice reminds pilgrims that Ibrahim was willing to sacrifice his son at God's command. Sheep, goats, and camels are slaughtered according to Islamic laws in the massive and very modern Mina abattoirs.

The Mosque in the Holy Haram

Finally the pilgrims return to Mecca. Here they circle the Kaaba once again before retiring to pray in the Holy Mosque by Al-Safa, within the Sacred Enclosure. This mosque is the most important point of the

▲ *Collecting stones on the mountain slopes at Mina*

▲ *Thousands of Muslims bowed in prayer at the Kaaba.*

city for Meccans. Apart from praying here whenever they can, they use it as a meeting place for most of the year. During the hajj period it is, of course, very crowded.

Thousands of worshipers throng the circular, tiled open space around the Kaaba to pray. Around 500,000 people can fit into the Sacred Enclosure at any one time. The cost each year of cleaning and maintaining the hajj complex is enormous, yet plans to rebuild and redecorate continue.

The government has plans to expand into the Suq al-Saghir (small market) area next to the Sacred Enclosure. Work is in progress on 100,000 square feet of this space.

Key words

testimony declaration

inscriptions markings or engravings

The Road Well Traveled

Each year, more than one million pilgrims crowd Mecca to worship at the sacred sites. The followers of Islam believe that those who accomplish this journey will receive spiritual rewards, and those who visit Mecca are given the honor of having the title *hajji* ("pilgrim") added to their name as a sign of honor.

Life in Mecca

Work and prayer

Once the pilgrims have left, Meccans can go back to their normal lives. Each morning at the break of dawn they hear the muezzin (crier) call them to prayer. All over Mecca people wake up, perform *wudu* (ritual cleansing), and prepare for their morning prayers. Men go to one of the many mosques, while women generally pray at home. Then they go to work until lunchtime.

It is impressive to see the people of Mecca stop their activities to answer *idhan*, the muezzin's call to prayer. Wafting across the city five times a day, the chant is a sound that is inseparable from Islam. Five times each day the city virtually comes to a halt as everyone spends a few minutes in prayer. People pray anywhere if they cannot go to a mosque: in offices, stores, and even on the sidewalks.

Eating and relaxing

Lunch, the main meal of the day, consists of meat, rice, and vegetables. Meccans, like all Arabs, love a fresh, crisp salad with their meal. Their desserts are generally cooling and milky. They are often flavored with rose water. Arab pastries, crisp and flaky, are famous around the world. They are often filled with a mixture of ground pistachio and other nuts and soaked in syrup. The meal is eaten in true Muslim tradition; anyone who is there is welcome to join.

Mecca becomes slow and drowsy in the midday heat. Most shops and offices are air-conditioned, but people prefer to remain at home. They close their shutters or draw the curtains to keep out the heat and the glare of the sun. Some take afternoon naps. Others just relax, wiling away the hot hours chatting together or watching television or a movie. As the sun passes the highest point in the sky, Meccans rise and prepare for the third prayer session of the day.

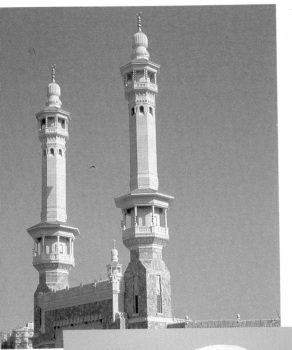

◀ *Muezzins make the call to prayer from tall minarets.*

Praying at home on a prayer mat that is pointed toward the Kaaba ▼

A basket of fresh fruit ▶

A dish of snacks, including olives and radishes ▼

▲ Tea is taken in the shade.

◄ Shopping in the market in the late afternoon

people love them and get together to celebrate with a traditional dish of rice and lentils.

The people of Mecca

Modern Meccans are of many different origins. Most have connections with some of the oldest tribes of the Hijaz. Some of these were once visitors to the city, but have now settled and lived here for many generations. There are Muslims from Africa, India, Indonesia, and Central Asia around Afghanistan and Russia. These different peoples tend to cluster into their own areas in the city. Although they have come from distant countries, their beliefs and practices are the same as those of other Meccans.

Family life is very important to Meccans. Parents show great love and affection to their children. In return, children are expected to respect and honor their parents. The Meccan household often consists of an extended family; grandparents, uncles, aunts, and cousins may all live in one house. Or they may live next to each other. Young couples today often choose to live in their own apartments. Family members continue to meet often and provide support for one another. When parents become old, their children look after them.

People begin to emerge from their homes in the late afternoon and the city buzzes with life. As the day goes on the temperature cools. Shops open at around 5:00 P.M. and stay open until as late as 10:30 at night.

In this desert city where rains are rare, people make the best of the cooler hours. Families make their way to the parks and playgrounds in the suburbs. At weekends they go farther afield into the neighboring mountains of Taif. Some people may drive over to Arafat for an evening picnic. Unlike people in cold countries, Meccans enjoy cloudy weather. When it does rain in Mecca, the rains are fierce and can cause floods. Yet

▲ Meccans are Muslims from many different parts of the world.

Festivals

Islamic festivals have a very special meaning for the people of Mecca, because most of them mark events that took place in and around their city. It is a matter of honor and pride for them to know that their city is remembered by a billion Muslims all over the world during these festivals.

The Islamic year follows the lunar calendar (see page 17), so Muslim festivals are not fixed. Each lunar month lasts for 29 or 30 days. This makes the lunar calendar 11 days shorter than the **solar calendar**, which has 365 days in each year. So each Muslim festival is celebrated 11 days earlier than the year before. This means that over a number of years, festivals occur in different seasons.

▲ Drums are beaten outside a mosque in Morocco during the Night of Power.

▼ Shopping for food at night during Ramadan

▲ Dancing is a traditional way of celebrating in Saudi Arabia.

Ramadan

Ramadan is one of the holiest months in the Islamic calendar. This was the month in which the Prophet Muhammad first saw the Angel Gabriel and began to receive the Word of God. During this month, Muslims neither eat nor drink between sunrise and sunset. While they fast, they are meant to pray and try their hardest to be good. Children are expected to fast from about the age of eleven. People who are ill do not fast. Restaurants are closed during the day in Ramadan and the whole city slows down. *Lailat-ul-Qadr* (The Night of Power) marks the exact time when the Koran was first revealed. It occurs during the last ten days of Ramadan. This time is set aside as a public holiday for people to pray and celebrate.

Mecca changes dramatically during Ramadan. It is transformed into a city of the night. After breaking their fast at sundown, people stay awake until the early hours, feasting, visiting friends, and praying. Shops are open all night, so people can conveniently get their shopping done at the same time. As dawn approaches they eat the meal that has to last them until sunset. Then they say their morning prayers and sleep for a while.

Id-ul-Fitr

As Ramadan draws to a close, people peer eagerly into the sky to catch sight of the thin crescent moon which shows that the new month is about to begin. On the next day, the festival of *Id-ul-Fitr* will be celebrated. Religious officials in Mecca announce when the new moon has been sighted. This information is sent to mosques around the world so that all Muslim countries can celebrate *Id* on the same day. *Id-ul-Fitr* is a public holiday.

Id day begins with an early morning visit to the mosque for communal prayer. Afterward people visit friends and relatives. They feast throughout the day. Dates and milk are served to everyone and children are given gifts of money and candy. Money is also given to different charities to help the poor and the sick.

Id-ul-Adha

The most important holy festival for the Muslims is *Id-ul-Adha*, the feast of the sacrifice. This occurs at the end of the hajj on the tenth day of Dhu'l-Hijja, the twelfth month of the Islamic year. After the excitement of the hajj, Meccans are content to celebrate this *Id* fairly quietly.

Key word

solar calendar following the cycle of the earth moving around the sun

It's a Date

The Islamic calendar is calculated using the cycles of the moon, while the Christian calendar follows the cycle of the sun.

Saudi children have painted the ways in which they celebrate festivals.

▲ *Sheep being herded onto a ship at Port Sudan. They will be transported to Saudi Arabia for the hajj.*

A focus for Muslims

Since the beginning of Islam, Muslims have looked to Mecca for spiritual leadership. As a result, Mecca became the first important center of Islamic religious study. Students from Muslim countries all over the world thronged to Mecca to study under the guidance of leading specialists in Islamic law. They were organized into groups, each one led by a **scholar**. The students assembled in the buildings of the Great Mosque around the Kaaba. As the number of students increased, the buildings began to overflow. Scholars opened their own homes to their students. These schools were known as the *katatib*. Reading, writing, grammar, and Islamic studies were all taught here. This tradition continues today.

There are several schools and universities in Mecca. They teach many different subjects; everything from English to engineering.

Islamic studies are still an important part of education. Children start to learn about religion when they begin school at the age of six. They are taught about Islam and how this affects their lives. Older students of Islam study at a College of Sharia and Islamic Studies, which is part of the Ummul Qura University in Mecca. Over the centuries, many students who came to study never returned home. They preferred to be near the Holy Haram.

The long tradition of Islamic studies in Mecca makes the scholars very important. They advise the rest of the country on its national laws. Saudi Arabia is the only country whose laws are entirely based on the Koran. Every new rule or law must agree with the Koran. Many of the scholars who check these are from Mecca.

Law and order in Mecca is excellent. People can leave their shops open when they stop for prayers without fear of anything

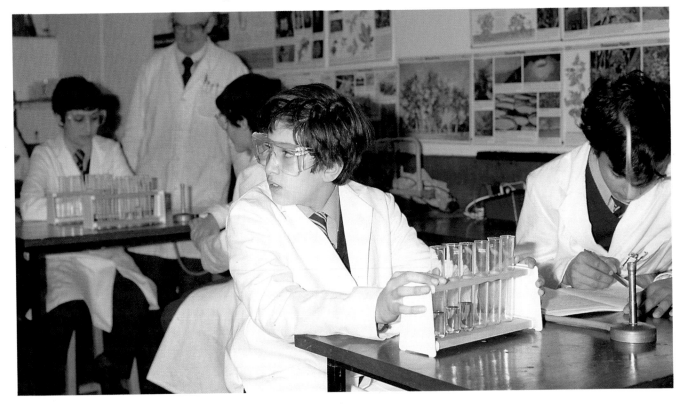

▲ *Students study science in a typical classroom.*

▲ *Students playing sports*

The flag and emblem of Saudi Arabia ▶

being stolen. There is very little street crime. All arguments are settled according to the laws set out in the Koran. Special ministries and government departments have been set up to look after the needs of different groups of people. *Zakaat*, or money for charity, is collected by the local government and spent on people who cannot provide for themselves.

Islam is such an important part of life in Saudi Arabia that the national flag proclaims the words, "There is no God but Allah, and Muhammad is the Messenger of Allah." This flag flies at all the ports and boundaries of the country and is never lowered to half-mast because of the sacred message on it.

Saudi rulers are proud that Mecca is within the boundaries of their country. They have worked hard over the years to try to establish a truly Islamic state. They feel that this is their duty because Mecca is the focus for Muslims all over the world.

Key word

scholar a studious, educated person

The Letter of the Law

There is no official constitution of Saudi Arabia, since most matters are decided by the laws contained in the Koran. If something is not covered in the Koran (traffic laws, for example), then the king issues a decree containing his decision.

Art and architecture

The shapes of the desert

The Arabs were among the first people to use abstract art. In this style of art, shapes or symbols are used to show what an artist sees, instead of the shapes of the objects themselves. A series of circles may represent a bunch of flowers. A rectangular brush stroke may symbolize a building.

Astronomy and mathematics were very important to Meccans. This is why **geometric** shapes of all kinds can be seen in so many examples of Islamic art. The desert is often represented by these shapes. The Meccans, with their desert links, loved their environment—the open skies, the vast stretches of flat desert broken by sand dunes, the oases with their cool, sparkling water and clusters of palms. The dome of the mosque symbolizes the sky; the minarets resemble the tall palms reaching for the heavens. Patterns

▲ *Patterned carpets, tiles, and plasterwork decorate the inside of this traditional Saudi house.*

on Arab carpets depict trees, water, the desert, sun, moon, and stars. Flowers, dates, and other fruits also appear.

◄ *Detail of a Bedouin tent cloth*

An elaborately patterned Saudi Arabian carpet ▼

Calligraphy

Islamic ornamental writing also came from the Arabs. It is known as calligraphy and is often used to decorate the pages of the Koran. Some of these special Korans are so stunning that they are on show in museums around the world. Real gold dust and gemstones such as lapis lazuli are used to make rich colors for the borders of the pages. Korans and books decorated in this way are known as illuminated manuscripts.

One of the first ornamental **scripts** was developed in Mecca around 651 C.E. about the time when the Koran was collected together. It was named the *Makki* script, after the name Mecca. The Makki script is very similar to the Kufic script, which is the most famous one today. Its vertical pen strokes are short and its horizontal strokes are long.

In time, calligraphy began to appear on the walls of mosques, both outside and inside. Verses from the Koran were written or carved inside different shapes that used **flourishes** and **scrolls**. These came to be known as *arabesques*. Calligraphers became very skilled in their art. They used the script to make pictures of ships, minarets, and various birds and animals. Human figures are not allowed in Islamic art. After the death of Muhammad, his followers did not want pictures or statues of humans made. They thought that this might encourage people to worship idols again. But the lack of human figures does not make Islamic art any less interesting. The most breathtaking examples are found in mosques from Spain in the west, to Indonesia and Brunei in the Far East.

The Sacred Mosque

The Sacred Mosque facing the Kaaba has changed many times over the years. It began life as a small roofless temple with walls of stone surrounding the Zam-zam well (see pages 8 and 30). In 608 C.E. it was repaired by a carpenter on his way to Abyssinia on a Byzantine ship. He rebuilt it with a mixture of stone and wood and painted pictures of flowers, trees, angels, and prophets on its ceiling and walls. He also painted the six columns holding up the building. The number of columns in the Sacred Mosque changed many times during the following years. One alteration left it with three large columns and another with more than 500!

Some years after the death of Muhammad, Khalifa Omar bought the large stone mansions around the Kaaba from their wealthy owners and created a space for prayer. Other khalifas added teaching and living quarters for those who served and worked in the Haram. One architect came all the way from Persia. He added touches of Persian design to the mosque, making it a grand and highly decorated building. Then an Omayyid khalifa pulled it down, replacing it with an oblong structure much more like the Prophet's own house. But later, the Ottoman Turks, famous for their magnificent mosques and beautiful forms of art, glorified the building once again. Today it is a breathtaking place, with walls of different colored marble, highly decorated pulpits, fine metal grilles of brass and **ornate** plaster work. Its **arcades** are held up with many beautiful arches and columns for which Islamic buildings are famous.

More mosques

Other mosques in Mecca have the same basic structure as those throughout the rest of the world. They are modeled on the design of the Prophet's house, having an open courtyard surrounded by arcades. The *mihrab*, an alcove in the wall facing the direction of the Kaaba, represents the Kaaba itself and is often highly decorated. The *mimbar* is the pulpit from

▲ *Calligraphy and symbols on a doorway*

▲ *Calligraphy showing arabesques*

▲ The spectacular mosque in Brunei, Southeast Asia

◄ A decorated tile panel in Topkapi Palace, Istanbul

which the *imam* (priest) preaches and recites verses of the Koran. Cleanliness is an important part of Islam. Muslims have to wash in a special way before they say prayers, so every mosque has a washing area. At the mosque door, rows of shoes clutter the entrance. Muslims have to take off their shoes before they enter their place of worship.

Key words

geometric shaped according to mathematical calculations, such as triangles

scripts styles of handwriting

flourishes bold strokes of the pen

scrolls coils and curls made with the pen

ornate highly decorated

arcades rows of arches

The changing face of Mecca

The rest of Mecca is very different in character from the Sacred Enclosure. It used to be a city of buildings radiating in a circle from around the Kaaba and the prayer space next to it. The grand mansions were so close to the Kaaba that their shadows merged at dusk and dawn. These mansions walled in the Kaaba, leaving hardly any prayer space around it. The Kaaba could only be reached through small streets running between the houses. These were known as the "gates" of the Holy Haram and were named after the important clans of Mecca.

The city was built so that the hot sun was kept out as much as possible. The busy and colorful markets were covered to keep them cool. Mecca was filled with narrow, shady lanes. The houses had walls of thick stone with long, narrow latticed windows to shut out the fiery sun.

Houses and apartments
Family members liked to live close to each other. So, as the family increased, new homes

▲ *Small clusters of houses on the outskirts of Mecca*

were built beside the old family home, forming small clusters of houses. Those who could afford it lived in one large mansion. Traditional Arab houses were built around a large open space. This meant that the family could be private while sitting in the open, enjoying the cooler hours of the day. A flat, walled terrace roof now replaces this in many modern houses. The magnificent mountain scenery is often visible from the rooftops.

When the demand for oil increased, Saudi Arabians had more money and were able to redesign Mecca. Many beautiful old buildings of architectural value were pulled down. New houses and apartment buildings were built away from the center of the city. With their thinner walls and modern doors and windows they are not so well suited to the hot, dry climate of Mecca. But most houses and apartments in Mecca are air-conditioned, so the heat is not a great problem anymore.

Markets and gardens
Two large amusement parks have been built in central Mecca. They are the Zahir Gardens and the Masfalah Gardens. The new suburbs have their own small gardens and parks.

▼ *Old, narrow lanes look out on to a modern building in Mecca.*

43 —

Arabic carving and plasterwork on buildings in Saudi Arabia

They also have large shopping arcades and supermarkets similar to those in Europe. Luckily, some of the old markets still survive. They are still very popular, especially for buying fresh fruits and vegetables. Both open and covered market places still thrive. They sell all manner of goods. The Souq al-Leyl just outside the Sacred Mosque is a very famous one. The original fruit and vegetable market is in the Jarwal district of Mecca. The districts of Ajyad, Shubaika, and Masfalah all have their own traditional market places.

▼ *Gardens like this have been made in Mecca and in cities throughout Saudi Arabia.*

Conservation

Modern architects in Mecca realize that the original design of the city was more suited to its surroundings than the modern one. Hopefully this means that the older buildings will be preserved from now on. Perhaps future planning will even include some older style constructions.

No doubt there will be many more changes and developments in this remarkable city. But one fact will never change. It will always be the most holy and magnetic city to millions of Muslims around the world, because at its heart is the Holy Haram, which the faithful long to visit in order to fulfill their spiritual dreams.

Important events in the history of Mecca

The following are some important events with the dates on which they occurred:

C.E. (A.D.)

571 Muhammad is born into Hashemite clan, related to the powerful tribe of Quraysh, which guards the Kaaba

609 Muhammad receives revelations on Mount Hira and begins preaching. His followers know he is the Prophet of God.

622 Holy Prophet and his followers move to Medina. Their journey is known as the Hegira.

624 Small Muslim army defeats Meccan troops at Badr oasis

627 Prophet's followers push back Meccan troops at Medina

628 Muhammad signs Treaty of Hudaybiya with Mecca, giving Prophet the right to make a pilgrimage, or hajj in 629

630 Muslim army, led by the Prophet, captures Mecca

632 Muhammad dies

632–661 Prophet's close companions become khalifas (leaders). They destroy buildings around Kaaba to make space for prayer area. Mecca becomes capital of Arabia.

644–656 Khalifa Uthman orders publication of Koran. It is sent to mosques.

650 Kaaba is rebuilt after fire

661 Last of the four companions of the Prophet is killed

661–750 Omayyad khilafat dominates Muslim world

670 Kaaba is rebuilt in old style

683 Black Stone cracked by fire

711–715 North African Muslims advance into Spain and northern Europe

750–1100 Abbasid khilafat of Baghdad takes over from Omayyads

789–809 Mecca is captured by Iraqi Muslim group. Black Stone is removed.

951 Remains of Black Stone returned to Kaaba and set in silver

968–1171 Muslim culture flourishes under Egyptian Fatimid ruling dynasty

1258 Muslim Mongols invade Baghdad. Abbasids collapse

1258 Mamluks rule in Egypt

1453 Ottoman empire is founded and conquers Constantinople (Istanbul)

1517 Ottomans defeat Mamluks and take over Egypt and Hijaz

1585 Ottoman empire declines

1805 Muhammad Wahhab and followers, under Muhammad Ibn Saud, take over Mecca

1810–1818 Muhammad Ali tries to rid Mecca of Wahhabis

1882–1850s Great Britain takes over Ottoman empire

1916 Muslim Arabs take over Mecca from Ottomans

1919 Mecca is no longer Arabia's capital

1919–1924 Abdul Aziz Ibn Saud wins battle in Hijaz and takes Mecca

1926 Ibn Saud is made King of Hijaz

1932 Hijaz Kingdom renamed Saudi Arabia

1965 Station of Ibrahim is made smaller and enclosed. Zam-zam well is opened up. New Saudi mosque is built around old Ottoman one.

Further Reading

Ali, Maureen. *Middle East*. Madison, New Jersey:
Raintree-Steck Vaughn, 1988.

Cairns, Trevor, ed. *Barbarians, Christians and Muslims*.
Minneapolis: Lerner Books, 1975.

Makhlouf, Georgia. *The Rise of Major Religions*.
Morristown, New Jersey: Silver-Burdett Press, 1988.

McCarthy, Kevin. *Saudi Arabia, A Desert Kingdom*.
New York: Dillon Press, 1989.

Morris, Scott, ed. *Religions of the World*. New York:
Chelsea House, 1993.

Morrison, Ian. *Middle East*. Madison, New Jersey:
Raintree-Steck Vaughn, 1991.

Index